With love to our little angel, Zach
~ Mimi

THE WISE ANIMAL HANDBOOK

Kate B. Jerome

ARCADIA KIDS

Attempt
new
skills
from
time
to
time.

Just **try** to think them **through.**

And if you find you're left behind...

...then
change
your point
of view.

Try not to think of just yourself.

Invent new ways to share.

Stay close to friends whom you can trust.

But
always
be
aware.

Avoid the tattle in the tale.

Insist that **truth** is **best.**

Embrace with pride the strengths you have.

Demand
to be
impressed.

Enjoy
the
peace
that
nature
brings.

Ignore what's just for show.

Join **forces** when the road gets **rough.**

Admit
when you
don't know.

Remember
family
is the
best.

Despite the ups and downs.

Don't **hide** from things that you must **face.**

Make
joyful
laughing
sounds.

Eat
healthy
food to
grow
up
strong.

Be **patient** with your friends.

Try not to take a stubborn stand.

Be
quick
to make
amends.

Excuse
yourself
when
manners
slip.

Be helpful every day.

Keep **trying** even when it's **hard.**

But
don't
forget to
play!

And
sing

...and **dance** each **day!**

Written by Kate B. Jerome
Design and Production: Lumina Datamatics, Inc.
Coloring Illustrations: Tom Pounders
Research: Eric Nyquist

Cover Images: See back cover

Interior Images: 002 Anetapics/Shutterstock.com; 003 George Green/Shutterstock.com; 004 Sergey Uryadnikov/Shutterstock.com; 005 Gnomeandi/Shutterstock.com; 006 Bruce MacQueen/Shutterstock.com; 007 Henk Bentlage/Shutterstock.com; 008 M.M./Shutterstock.com; 009 Mikael Damkier/Shutterstock.com; 010 Brendan van Son/Shutterstock.com; 011 Michael Pettigrew/Shutterstock.com; 012 StevenRussellSmithPhotos/Shutterstock.com; 013 Pakhnyushchy/Shutterstock.com; 014 Patjo/Shutterstock.com; 015 Quinn Martin/Shutterstock.com; 016 Lincoln Rogers/Shutterstock.com; 017 Dirk Ercken/Shutterstock.com; 018 Karel Gallas/Shutterstock.com; 019 Orangecrush/Shutterstock.com; 020 Guenter-foto/Shutterstock.com; 021 Janecat/Shutterstock.com; 022 Shironina/Shutterstock.com; 023 Annette Shaff/Shutterstock.com; 024 Vitaly Titov/Shutterstock.com; 025 Rohappy/Shutterstock.com; 026 MattiaATH/Shutterstock.com; 027 Otsphoto/Shutterstock.com; 028 FikMik/Shutterstock.com; 029 Four Oaks/Shutterstock.com; 030 Ekaterina Kolomeets/Shutterstock.com; 031 Hugh Lansdown/Shutterstock.com.

Published by Arcadia Kids, a division of Arcadia Publishing and
The History Press, Charleston, SC

For all general information contact Arcadia Publishing at:
Telephone: 843-853-2070
Email: sales@arcadiapublishing.com

For Customer Service and Orders:
Toll Free: 1-888-313-2665
Visit us on the Internet at www.arcadiapublishing.com

Library of Congress Cataloging-in-Publication data is on file with the publisher.

Printed in China

Massachusetts State Bird

Black-Capped Chickadee

Read Together

The black-capped chickadee was named the state bird in 1941. Unlike other birds, black-capped chickadees do not fly south for the winter.

Massachusetts State Cat

Tabby Cat

Read Together

The tabby cat was voted the state cat in 1988 to honor the wishes of Massachusetts schoolchildren from across the state.

Massachusetts State Dog

Boston Terrier

Read Together

The Boston terrier was named the state dog in 1979. It was the first pure bred dog "made" in America!

Massachusetts State Game Bird

Wild Turkey

Read Together: The wild turkey was named the state game bird in 1991. Conservation efforts in the last 30 years have helped the wild turkey population grow across the state.